KEY PEOPLE
OF THE REVOLUTIONARY WAR

PATRICK CATEL

Heinemann Library
Chicago, Illinois

MAR 2011

www.heinemannraintree.com
Visit our website to find out more information about Heinemann-Raintree books.

To order:
☎ Phone 888-454-2279
💻 Visit www.heinemannraintree.com to browse our catalog and order online.

©2011 Heinemann Library
an imprint of Capstone Global Library, LLC
Chicago, Illinois

Edited by Megan Cotugno
Designed by Ryan Frieson
Picture research by Tracy Cummins
Originated by Capstone Global Library
Printed and bound in China by CTPS

14 13 12 11 10
10 9 8 7 6 5 4 3 2 1

Library of Congress Cataloging-in-Publication Data

Catel, Patrick.
  Key people of the Revolutionary War / Patrick Catel.
    p. cm. — (Why we fought : the Revolutionary War)
  Includes bibliographical references and index.
  ISBN 978-1-4329-3897-0 (hc)—ISBN 978-1-4329-3902-1 (pb)
  1. United States—History--Revolution,
1775-1783—Biography—Juvenile literature. 2. United States—History—Revolution, 1775-1783—Juvenile literature. I. Title.
  E206.C39 2011
  973.3—dc22
                    2009050074

Acknowledgments

The author and publishers are grateful to the following for permission to reproduce copyright material:

Corbis pp. 8, 10, 13 bottom, 19, 25 (© Bettman); Getty Images pp. 12 (Hulton Archive), 38 (Stock Montage); Library of Congress Prints and Photographs Division pp. 5, 6, 9 bottom, 11, 13 top, 14, 17, 18, 21, 24, 29, 36, 37, 41, 42, 43; National Archives pp. 4, 23; The Art Archive p. 15 (National Gallery of Art Washington); The Bridgeman Art Library International pp. 7 (© Collection of the New-York Historical Society, USA), 16, 32 (Peter Newark American Pictures), 26, 30 (© Look and Learn), 31 (R. Bayne Powell Collection), 33 (National Army Museum, London), 34, 35; The Granger Collection, New York pp. 9 top, 22, 27, 28, 39, 40.

Cover photo of George Washington reproduced with permission from The Art Archive (Gift of John Hill Morgan/ Museum of the City of New York / 46.1a). Cover photo of portrait of King George III reproduced with permission from Getty Images (Allan Ramsay).

We would like to thank Dr. Edward Cook for his invaluable help in the preparation of this book.

Contents

Throughout this book, you will find green text boxes that contain facts and questions to help you interact with a primary source. Use these questions as a way to think more about where our historical information comes from.

Some words are shown in bold, **like this**. You can find out what they mean by looking in the glossary, on page 46.

Why Did We Fight the Revolutionary War?

Today, the United States of America is known as one of the strongest nations in the world. This can make it difficult to imagine how close the **colonies** were to failing in their revolution. Americans risked their lives in a revolt against the most powerful nation in the world. Why would the colonists risk so much?

In 1760, George III became king of Great Britain. He signed the Treaty of Paris with France in 1763 to end the **French and Indian War**. The British gained control of Canada and the land east of the Mississippi River. However, Great Britain had a large debt from the war.

Primary Source: The Declaration of Independence

In 1775, this document was written to explain why the colonists wanted independence from Great Britain. On July 4, 1776, it was signed by 56 members of Congress.

Thinking About the Source:

What materials do you think were used to create this document?

Do you think the same materials would be used if it was created today?

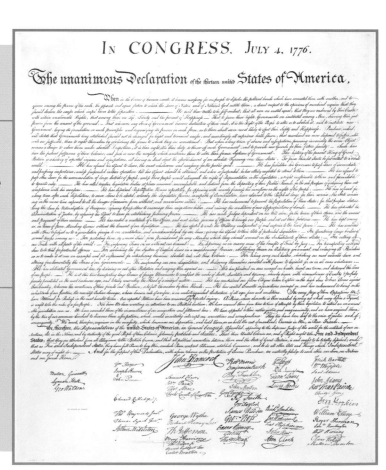

British Taxes

King George III and the British **Parliament** felt colonists in North America should help pay for the French and Indian War and the protection provided by British troops. Great Britain began to pass acts (laws) that required the colonists to pay taxes. These included the **Sugar Act** in 1764, the **Stamp Act** in 1765, the **Townshend Acts** in 1767, the **Tea Act** in 1773, and the **Intolerable Acts** in 1774. The colonies responded by protesting and boycotting (refusing to buy) British goods. Colonists also formed groups such as the **Sons of Liberty** to take action against the acts.

Events turned violent in Boston in 1770, when British troops fired on a rowdy crowd that was protesting British policies. Samuel Adams called it the "Boston Massacre." Support grew for the cause of colonial independence. The more colonists protested, the more King George III refused to budge. The king ordered the use of military force to keep control in Massachusetts. In 1775, months before the signing of the Declaration of Independence, the Revolutionary War had already begun.

The Declaration of Independence was signed in 1776, months after the first fighting of the war had taken place.

John Adams (1735–1826)

John Adams first worked as a teacher and then decided to become a lawyer. In 1764, he married Abigail Smith (see page 38). John and Abigail Adams wrote each other many letters during the times they were apart. John Adams served in the first and second **Continental Congresses**. He was part of the committee that drafted the Declaration of Independence. Adams accepted appointment as a diplomat (representative) and sailed to France in 1778 with his son, John Quincy, who was ten years old. Adams spent most of the Revolutionary War in France. He helped **negotiate** the Treaty of Paris, which ended the Revolutionary War in 1783.

After the War

John Adams was appointed minister to Great Britain in 1785. In 1789, he was selected as the first vice president of the United States. In 1796, he was elected the second president of the United States. Adams lost the 1800 election to Thomas Jefferson. John Adams and Thomas Jefferson were friends, but also bitter rivals. However, they ended life as friends. Both died on July 4, 1826.

As a lawyer, John Adams defended the British soldiers accused in the Boston Massacre.

Samuel Adams (1722–1803)

Samuel Adams was the leader of the **colonial** opposition to British policies in Massachusetts. He helped organize the **Sons of Liberty** in Boston. He helped lead the resistance to the **Stamp Act** and **Townshend Acts**. Adams also led the fight against paying the tax on tea and encouraged the Boston Tea Party in 1773. He was selected as a **delegate** to the first and second Continental Congresses. Adams was elected governor of Massachusetts in 1793. He died in Boston in 1803.

Samuel Adams argued that the Sugar Act of 1764 violated the rights of colonists because it had not been created with the approval of an elected representative from the colonies. He said that there should be "no taxation without representation." This was a popular saying among the colonists who were fighting for independence.

Ethan Allen
(1738–1789)

Ethan Allen was the fearless commander of the Green Mountain Boys. They were a fighting group formed to keep New Yorkers from settling on Vermont land. In 1775, Ethan Allen and Benedict Arnold captured Fort Ticonderoga from the British. They took 45 prisoners and many valuable supplies. On September 25, 1775, the British captured Allen near Montreal, Canada. He was eventually returned to the **colonies** in a prisoner exchange. In 1787, Allen settled in Burlington, Vermont. He died there in 1789.

Ethan Allen became a hero because of his actions at Fort Ticonderoga.

James Armistead (1760–1832)

James Armistead was a slave. He got permission from his owner to join the Continental Army. In 1781, the Marquis de Lafayette asked Armistead to pretend he wanted to help the British. The British believed him. Armistead sent information about British troops back to the Continental Army. After a time, British General Cornwallis asked Armistead to spy on Lafayette. Armistead gave false information to the British while continuing to spy for the **Patriots**. After the Revolutionary War, in 1786, Armistead finally received his freedom

James Armistead added "Lafayette" to his name after the Revolutionary War, in honor of the French leader.

HERO AND TRAITOR: BENEDICT ARNOLD (1741–1801)

Benedict Arnold was a Patriot military leader at the beginning of the Revolutionary War. He forced the surrender of Fort Ticonderoga in 1775. He blocked the British advance at the Battle of Valcour Island in 1776, and he helped defeat the British at Saratoga in 1777. However, Arnold became unhappy that he was not receiving enough credit and higher positions (jobs) in the army.

Arnold eventually grew angry enough to become a spy for the British. George Washington did not know this. He appointed Arnold commander of West Point in New York. Arnold planned to hand over this military post to the British. John André, a major in the British Army, was captured with papers describing the plan. However, Arnold escaped and fought for the British for the rest of the war.

Crispus Attucks (c. 1723–1770)

Crispus Attucks was a former slave who worked on whaling ships. On March 5, 1770, a protest against the British in Boston turned violent. British soldiers fired their weapons. Attucks and four others in the crowd were killed in what became known as the Boston Massacre. Attucks was one of the first Americans to die in the fight against Great Britain.

GEORGE ROGERS CLARK (1752–1818) AND THE FRONTIER

During the Revolutionary War, the land west of the **colonies**, closer to the Mississippi River, was considered the western **frontier**. The British encouraged Native Americans to raid (attack) settlements in this territory. George Rogers Clark led a small army into the frontier. They attacked British outposts and Native-American villages in what is now considered the Midwestern United States. Clark's success made sure that the frontier territory went to the Americans in the Treaty of Paris at the end of the war.

Benjamin Franklin (1706–1790)

Benjamin Franklin settled in Philadelphia, where he owned a newspaper called the *Pennsylvania Gazette*. Franklin published *Poor Richard's Almanack* from 1732 to 1757. An almanac is a book arranged like a calendar that is published once a year. It contains facts about many different subjects, including the weather. Franklin also wrote poems and wise sayings in his almanacs, which were popular books.

Benjamin Franklin served in the Pennsylvania Assembly from 1751 to 1764. Frankiin also spent many years in Great Britain as a spokesman for the colonies. In 1775, Franklin represented Pennsylvania in the second **Continental Congress**. He was also a member of the committee chosen to write the Declaration of Independence. Franklin later traveled to France to get financial and military assistance for the colonies. He was also in France to help **negotiate** the peace treaty to end the Revolutionary War. Franklin returned to Philadelphia and helped write the United States Constitution in 1787.

Primary Source: Benjamin Franklin

Benjamin Franklin was 69 years old and a talented statesman, or government leader, by the time the Revolutionary War began.

Thinking About the Source:

What do you notice first about this portrait?

Who do you think was the audience for this image?

Nathanael Greene
(1742–1786)

At age 32, Nathanael Greene was the youngest general in the Continental Army. Greene fought in several battles in the North. He then took command of the Continental Army in the South in 1780. He kept British General Cornwallis from capturing North Carolina. Greene then led his army into South Carolina and attacked British outposts. Greene eventually forced the British Army to retreat to Yorktown, Virginia. At Yorktown, the British surrendered to George Washington.

Nathan Hale
(1755–1776)

Nathan Hale was a teacher before joining the Connecticut militia when the Revolutionary War began. During the Battle of Long Island in 1776, Hale volunteered to spy on British troop movements. British forces captured him near present-day Queens in New York City. Nathan Hale was hanged for **treason** the next day, September 22, 1776.

Nathanael Greene was one of eight children in a Quaker family.

Alexander Hamilton (1757–1804)

Alexander Hamilton fought in battles around New York City in 1775 and 1776. He also led a regiment of New York troops at the Battle of Yorktown in 1781. Hamilton was elected a member of the **Continental Congress** in 1782. He also served as a New York delegate to the Constitutional Convention of 1787. Hamilton became the first secretary of the treasury in 1789. He created a national bank and organized the Treasury Department. Aaron Burr shot and killed Hamilton in a duel on July 11, 1804.

Alexander Hamilton was in favor of a strong national government, as opposed to giving more power to the states.

John Hancock was one of the wealthiest merchants in New England.

John Hancock (1737–1793)

John Hancock strongly supported independence from Great Britain. He became president of the Continental Congress in 1775. He was the first to sign the original Declaration of Independence on July 4, 1776. John Hancock's clear, fancy signature was a demonstration of patriotism, and Hancock became a symbol of the struggle for independence.

Patrick Henry (1736–1799)

Patrick Henry was born in Virginia. After studying law, he served in the Virginia **House of Burgesses**. He served five terms as governor of Virginia. Henry was a leader in the fight for independence from Great Britain, speaking out against British **tyranny** and supporting **colonial** rights. In March 1775, Patrick Henry ended a speech to his fellow Virginians with the famous words: "I know not what course others may take; but as for me, give me liberty or give me death."

John Jay (1745–1829)

John Jay wanted to avoid war and make peace with Great Britain. However, Jay supported independence once peace was not possible. He was a **delegate** to the **Continental Congress** in 1774 to 1776, and again in 1778. He was elected president of the Continental Congress in 1778. Jay served in other ways, including as the first Chief Justice of the Supreme Court. He was also governor of New York from 1795 to 1801.

Patrick Henry's words, "give me liberty or give me death," became a famous call for independence.

Thomas Jefferson (1743–1826)

Thomas Jefferson was the author of the Declaration of Independence. Jefferson served in the Virginia law-making body and was elected governor from 1779 to 1781. In 1784, he traveled to France as trade commissioner. Jefferson then took over for Benjamin Franklin as minister to France. In 1790, Jefferson became secretary of state under President George Washington. In 1796, he became vice president to John Adams after losing to him in a close presidential election.

Presidency and Later Life

In 1800, Thomas Jefferson defeated John Adams to become the third president of the United States. Jefferson served two terms. In 1803, during his first term, Jefferson purchased the **Louisiana Territory** from France. He then supported the Lewis and Clark expedition. Thomas Jefferson remained at Monticello, his home in Virginia, for the last 17 years of his life. He died on July 4, 1826, just hours before John Adams. The date was the 50th anniversary of the signing of the Declaration of Independence.

Thomas Jefferson is probably most famous as the author of the Declaration of Independence.

John Paul Jones (1747–1792)

John Paul Jones was a commander in the newly formed Continental Navy, and was one of its founders. He was born John Paul in Scotland in 1747. He took his first job at sea at age 12. In 1769, John Paul became captain of the British merchant ship *John*. During a **mutiny** on his ship, John Paul killed a sailor. To avoid a trial he thought would be unfair, John Paul fled to the American colonies. There he changed his name to John Paul Jones.

The *Bonhomme Richard* caught fire during the Battle of Flamborough Head. The British Captain Pearson called for John Paul Jones to surrender, but Jones refused.

During the War

During the Revolutionary War, Jones successfully captured British merchant ships. He also helped the war effort by raiding (attacking) British ports and ships. In 1779, Jones was promoted to **commodore** and given command of the *Bonhomme Richard*. He faced the British warship HMS *Serapis* on September 23, 1779, in the Battle of Flamborough Head. Jones's ship sank during the battle, but the British surrendered in the end.

James Madison (1751–1836)

James Madison was elected to Virginia's Revolutionary Convention in 1776. He wrote a document for freedom of religion in Virginia. Madison was sent to the **Continental Congress** in March 1780. At the Constitutional Convention in 1787, Madison earned the title "Father of the Constitution." This was because he provided many of the Constitution's main ideas. He also wrote many of the **Federalist papers**, which were published in newspapers. They promoted the ratification, or official approval, of the Constitution.

Madison was elected to the House of Representatives. He proposed the first ten amendments to the Constitution, also called the **Bill of Rights**. Madison was secretary of state when President Thomas Jefferson made the Louisiana Purchase in 1803. He served as the fourth president of the United States in 1809–1817. The **War of 1812** was fought during this time.

Primary Source:
James Madison

James Madison is known as the "Father of the Constitution."

Thinking about the source:

What details can you see in this image?

How does this portrait compare to the one of Benjamin Franklin (pg. 11)?

Francis Marion (1732–1795)

Francis Marion was nicknamed the "Swamp Fox" by the British. This was because of his ability to move and attack quickly and then slip away back into the southern swamps with his men. Marion and his men carried out daring raids and often defeated larger groups of British soldiers. Marion served in the senate of South Carolina after the war, from 1782 to 1790.

James Monroe (1758–1831)

James Monroe fought as an officer in the Continental Army during the Revolutionary War. He was severely wounded at the Battle of Trenton. After the war, Monroe studied law. He was then elected to the **Continental Congress** in 1783. Monroe was a United States senator before serving as minister to France from 1794 to 1796. In 1803, he helped **negotiate** the purchase of the **Louisiana Territory** for President Thomas Jefferson. Monroe served as the fifth president of the United States in 1817–1825. During his presidency, he declared what later became known as the **Monroe Doctrine**.

Thomas Paine (1737–1809)

In 1774, in London, England, Thomas Paine met Benjamin Franklin, who helped him come to the American **colonies**. Paine settled in Philadelphia and began a career as a journalist. On January 10, 1776, Paine published a short pamphlet called *Common Sense*. In *Common Sense*, Paine committed himself to the cause of American independence from Great Britain. His plain language appealed to the common people of America.

Hundreds of colonists read and knew about Thomas Paine's *Common Sense*. It helped the movement for independence gain support.

Paul Revere (1735–1818)

Paul Revere fought in the **French and Indian War** and supported the **Patriots** in the Revolutionary War. On the evening of April 18, 1775, Paul Revere and William Dawes left Boston to warn colonists in Lexington and Concord that the British were coming. Both Revere and Dawes were captured before reaching Concord. However, their warning stopped the British from finding the weapons and people they had set out to find.

Paul Revere was a silversmith and engraver by trade.

George Washington (1732–1799)

George Washington was born in Virginia. He learned to **survey** land at the age of 16, and inherited his own land at age twenty. Washington became a wealthy Virginia planter and businessman. In 1759, he married the widow Martha Dandridge Custis.

Washington served for 16 years in the Virginia **House of Burgesses**. He was also a representative for Virginia to the first and second **Continental Congresses**. Washington joined the Virginia **militia** in 1753. He gained valuable military experience fighting for the British in the **French and Indian War**. In 1774, he was again part of the Virginia militia. Washington was made commander in chief of the Continental Army in 1775.

Commander in Chief

When George Washington took command in 1775, he was faced with an unorganized group. It was made up of volunteer militiamen from all over the **colonies** and **frontier**. The men of the army were ready to fight, but they lacked training, discipline, and supplies. Washington used his leadership and military skills, along with the help of his commanders, to get the Continental Army into shape and ready for battle.

Washington convinced soldiers to continue the fight during many difficult times. His own efforts and self-sacrifice earned him the respect of his men. Washington also worked hard to convince political leaders to provide his soldiers with the supplies they badly needed. By making good command decisions at important points during the war, Washington managed to defeat the British Army, which was considered to be one of of the best armies in the world.

With the help of the French Army and Navy, Washington forced the British to surrender at Yorktown, Virginia, in 1781. This victory guaranteed independence for the colonists. George Washington was elected the first president of the United States of America in 1789. He served two terms, but turned down the opportunity to serve a third term.

George Washington was a tall man at 6 feet 2 inches and was inspiring to his troops. To share their sacrifice, Washington never accepted the salary that Congress offered him.

Bernardo de Galvez (1746–1786)

Bernardo de Galvez served with the Spanish Army. He became governor of Louisiana in 1777. There he supported the efforts of the Continental Army. Once Spain officially entered the war in support of American independence, Galvez took control of several British outposts on the Mississippi River. He captured Mobile in 1780 and Pensacola in 1781. Because of Galvez's efforts, Great Britain gave control of Florida and the mouth of the Mississippi River to Spain at the end of the Revolutionary War in 1783.

Bernardo de Galvez was born into a noble family in Spain.

Baron Johann de Kalb (1721–1780)

Johann Kalb (called Baron de Kalb) was born in what is now Germany in 1721. He left home at age 16. He was a lieutenant in the French military. De Kalb was sent to America in 1768 as a secret French agent. His mission was to find out how the **colonies** felt about the rule of Great Britain, France's long-time enemy. He returned to America in 1777, along with Lafayette. De Kalb spent the winter of 1777–1778 at Valley Forge with George Washington's army.

Fighting in the South

De Kalb was then assigned to relieve Charleston in South Carolina, but arrived too late. Horatio Gates was made commander of the southern part of the war, and de Kalb then served under him. During the Battle of Camden in 1780, de Kalb fought off Cornwallis's army. Gates and the **militia** fled the field, and eventually de Kalb's troops were also forced to retreat. Johann de Kalb was severely wounded in the fighting and died three days later.

Johann de Kalb was severely wounded during the Battle of Camden in 1780.

23

Thaddeus Kosciuszko (1746–1817)

Thaddeus Kosciuszko attended the Polish royal military school and the French army school. Kosciuszko came to America in 1776. The **Continental Congress** made him colonel of engineers in the Continental Army. Kosciuszko strengthened the defenses at battle sites, which often made the difference in a fight. He planned the defense for the **Patriot** victory at the Battle of Saratoga. Kosciuszko returned to Europe and fought for Polish independence. He returned to America in 1797 to a hero's welcome.

Gilbert du Motier, Marquis de Lafayette (1757–1834)

Gilbert du Motier was born in France to a wealthy noble family. He was orphaned, married, and entered military service all as a teenager. Lafayette sailed to America in 1777 to fight against the

Lafayette's full given name was Marie Joseph Paul Yves Roch Gilbert du Motier.

British. He paid for his own expenses and donated large amounts of his own money to the American cause. Lafayette trapped Cornwallis's army at Yorktown, where the British surrendered. He returned to the United States in 1824 and toured the country as a hero. The U.S. government granted him money and land as repayment for his contributions to the American Revolution.

Casimir Pulaski (1747–1779)

Casimir Pulaski was born into a noble family in Poland. He met Benjamin Franklin while in Paris. Franklin convinced him to go to America. Pulaski arrived in Boston in 1777. He served with Washington at the Battle of Brandywine. He proved his bravery there when he led a daring **cavalry** charge to cover the escape of Washington and his army.

The Continental Congress made Pulaski brigadier general and commander of the cavalry. In 1778, Pulaski resigned as commander. He formed his own cavalry, the "Pulaski Legion." Pulaski was severely wounded at the Battle of Savannah. He died two days later on October 11, 1779, aboard the American ship *Wasp*. The United States celebrates Casimir Pulaski Day on the first Monday of March to honor him.

Casimir Pulaski is sometimes called the "Father of the American Cavalry."

Comte de Rochambeau (1725–1807)

Jean-Baptiste Donatien de Vimeur, comte de Rochambeau, was born in France. By 1747, he was a colonel in the French Army. Rochambeau took part in battles in Europe and was wounded several times. He attained the rank of lieutenant general in 1780. Rochambeau was given command of the large French force sent to join the American colonists under George Washington. Together, along with the help of the French Navy, Rochambeau and Washington forced the British to surrender at the Battle of Yorktown in 1781.

Rochambeau also helped Washington's army by providing money from France.

ADMIRAL DE GRASSE AND THE FRENCH NAVY

Comte de Rochambeau and George Washington depended on the French Navy to force the British to surrender at Yorktown in 1781. The French fleet was under the command of Admiral Francois Joseph Paul, comte de Grasse. He defeated the British fleet off the coast of Virginia in September of 1781. Admiral de Grasse then positioned the French fleet of ships at Chesapeake Bay. This prevented Cornwallis and the British from escaping Yorktown by water. The British had no choice but to surrender.

Despite the fact that he spoke no English, Baron von Steuben successfully trained the American troops. He taught them military discipline and got them ready for battle.

Friedrich Wilhelm Augustus, Baron von Steuben (1730–1794)

Friedrich Wilhelm Augustus von Steuben, later Baron von Steuben, was born in Germany. By the time of the Revolutionary War, von Steuben was already a veteran of two wars. He met Benjamin Franklin in Paris, and he soon became a volunteer for the American cause of independence from Great Britain.

George Washington appointed von Steuben acting inspector general of the Continental Army in 1778. During the winter of 1777–1778 at Valley Forge, von Steuben organized and trained Washington's army. He also wrote the first American military manual (guidebook). He later fought at Yorktown at the end of the war. Von Steuben left the army in 1784. He stayed in America and retired in New York.

John André (1751–1780)

John André was with the British Army in Philadelphia. He became friends with Peggy Shippen, who married Benedict Arnold. André was put in charge of British spying activities. In 1780, Benedict Arnold offered to hand over West Point, an important fort, to the British. André met with Arnold and received documents from him. When he returned, André found that his ship was no longer on the Hudson River. He was forced to travel in disguise over land toward British troops. **Militiamen** stopped André, and they quickly discovered Arnold's papers. Since he was a spy, André was sentenced to death and was hanged.

John André only had 24 kilometers (15 miles) to go when he was captured. His captors quickly found Benedict Arnold's papers, which were hidden in André's boot.

Joseph Brant (1742–1807)

Joseph Brant was a Mohawk Indian born in Ohio. His birth name was Thayandanegea. Eventually Brant became a Mohawk Iroquois chief. As a young man, he fought alongside the British in the **French and Indian War**. During the Revolutionary War, Brant convinced many Mohawks and other Iroquois tribes to support the British. He also led raids on **Patriot** settlers. He wanted to keep them from taking more land from the Mohawks. After the Revolutionary War, Brant obtained land in Ontario, Canada. He was the leader of many Mohawk people there.

NATIVE AMERICANS IN THE REVOLUTION

Most Native Americans wanted to stay out of the conflict between the British and the colonists. Both sides tried to convince tribes to help. Native Americans were most concerned with settlers, who seemed to want more and more land. For that reason, most American Indians who fought sided with the British. Some did fight for the Continental Army, however. Some tribes were split by the war. Most Native Americans who supported the British hoped that, if the British won, they would help protect their way of life.

Primary Source: Joseph Brant, 1776

Joseph Brant's birth name, Thayandanegea, means "he places two bets."

Thinking About the Source:

What small details do you notice about the clothes that Brant is wearing?

Can you see any other details?

General John Burgoyne (1722–1792)

Before the Revolutionary War, John Burgoyne served in **Parliament.** He was sent to Boston in 1775 and returned to England several months later. He proposed a plan for a new invasion of New York. His idea was to split New England from the rest of the **colonies**. Burgoyne was placed in charge of the British forces in Canada. He arrived

there in 1777 and began his invasion plan. Burgoyne succeeded in retaking Fort Ticonderoga. However, he then faced several defeats. Burgoyne was finally forced to surrender to General Gates at Saratoga on October 17, 1777. This was the greatest defeat the British suffered in the Revolutionary War. Burgoyne returned to England. He never commanded British troops again.

General John Burgoyne was well liked by his men, because he always treated them with respect. They gave him the name "Gentleman Johnny" because of his firm but friendly and respectful nature.

BRITISH POLITICS

Some people in Parliament opposed the British government's actions against the colonies. William Pitt was one of these people. He was a former prime minister who had led the British government during the **French and Indian War**. In 1775, Pitt had an idea to help prevent war with the colonies. He suggested that the British let the Americans govern themselves through the **Continental Congress**, while still remaining a part of the British Empire. The idea was rejected, but Pitt continued to argue against British policies as the Revolutionary War continued.

Edmund Burke was another Member of Parliament who spoke out against British government policies toward the American colonies. He had spent some time in New York and understood why colonists were upset. In 1775, Burke argued for a more peaceful policy due to the value of trade with the colonies. He argued that the British taxes would be seen as a form of slavery by the colonists, even if they were legal. Like Pitt, Burke continued to speak out against British policies throughout the Revolutionary War.

Edmund Burke also spoke out for the **abolition** of the international slave trade.

General Sir Guy Carleton (1724–1808)

Sir Guy Carleton first served in the British Army in North America during the **French and Indian War**. When Thomas Gage resigned, Carleton was given command of the British forces in Canada. When fighting broke out in Massachusetts, Carleton sent his Canadian regulars, or professional British army soldiers, to Boston to help the British. Carleton was successful in defending Quebec against the American expedition of Benedict Arnold. With reinforcements from General John Burgoyne, Carleton led a successful counterattack. He pursued the defeated Americans into New York.

Carleton then had disagreements with his supervisors and was removed from command in 1777. He resigned as governor and left Canada in 1778. Carleton was made commander in chief of the British forces in the colonies in 1782, after the British had surrendered. His job was to stop the fighting and remove British forces. He also helped **Loyalists** leave their old homes.

Sir Guy Carleton was also the governor of Quebec, Canada, before and after the Revolutionary War.

Sir Henry Clinton (1738–1795)

Sir Henry Clinton began his service with the British Army in Great Britain. Clinton served in the **French and Indian War**. In 1772, he became a major general and a Member of Parliament. In 1775, Clinton came to Boston along with General Howe and General Burgoyne. Clinton served in the Battle of Bunker Hill and became second in command to General Howe. The British were upset that Howe was unable to win the war quickly.

In 1778, General Clinton replaced General Howe as commander in chief of the British forces in the American colonies. In 1780, he helped Cornwallis defeat the **Patriots** in Charleston before returning north to New York. However, after two more years of fighting, Clinton was also unable to completely defeat the colonists. He turned his command over to General Sir Guy Carleton and returned to England.

Sir Henry Clinton was born into a wealthy British family and raised in New York.

General Lord Charles Cornwallis (1738–1805)

Lord Charles Cornwallis joined the British Army in 1756 and served in the **French and Indian War**. He volunteered to come to the American **colonies** in 1776. Cornwallis fought in many battles in the northern colonies early in the war. In 1779, he sailed south with Henry Clinton. They defeated the **Patriots** at Charleston, South Carolina. Cornwallis then became the commander of the British Army in the southern colonies. He was successful in many battles in the South.

Cornwallis did have a hard time leading his troops against Continental riflemen in woodland battles, where the British soldiers often had to respond to surprise attacks. In 1781, Continental and French forces trapped Cornwallis and the British at Yorktown, Virginia. Cornwallis was forced to surrender. This was the last major battle of the Revolutionary War.

Cornwallis purchased his commission in the British Army, which was an acceptable way to become a British officer at the time.

General Thomas Gage (1721–1787)

Thomas Gage was a professional soldier in the British Army. He came to North America to serve in the French and Indian War. Gage became the first commander in chief of British forces in the North American colonies. He was appointed governor of

Massachusetts in 1774. In 1775, he sent troops to Concord to take or destroy weapons and ammunition there. The local militiamen resisted and exchanged fire with the British troops.

This marked the start of the Revolutionary War. Later that same year, Gage commanded the British Army at the Battle of Bunker Hill. Although Gage won the battle, he lost many troops. The British government was unhappy with him for failing to stop the **rebellion** altogether in the colonies. Gage was ordered to return to England.

General Thomas Gage planned, directed, and gave orders for the British attack on Bunker Hill, but he did not actually fight in the battle. Other military commanders, including Howe, carried out his orders on the battlefield.

"MAD KING GEORGE"—KING GEORGE III (1738–1820)

George III became King of Great Britain in 1760 at the age of 22. With the **Treaty of Paris** ending the **French and Indian War** in 1763, Great Britain was the world's greatest **colonial** power. However, Great Britain was in debt from the war. George III was determined to tax the colonies to pay for military protection. His refusal to change his mind eventually led to the Revolutionary War. George III suffered from a disease that caused him to experience periods of madness. Eventually, he was not able to make decisions.

Sir William Howe (1729–1814)

Sir William Howe was a successful leader in the British Army in North America during the French and Indian War. During the Revolutionary War, he was again ordered to go to North America, and he participated in the Battle of Bunker Hill in 1775. In 1776, Howe replaced General Thomas Gage as commander in chief of British forces in America. Howe captured New York City in 1776, and Philadelphia in 1777. However, British officials were still unhappy with him for failing to destroy Washington's Continental Army. In 1778, Howe resigned as commander in chief and returned to Britain.

John Pitcairn (1722–1775)

John Pitcairn was born in Scotland in 1722. In November 1774, Pitcairn arrived in Boston with about 600 British **marines**. Pitcairn commanded the troops sent to destroy the stored weapons and ammunition in Concord, Massachusetts. When they met the armed militia at Lexington, Pitcairn tried to prevent violence. However, shots were fired, and the Revolutionary War began. Pitcairn led his marines in an uphill charge at the Battle of Bunker Hill. He was hit by a musket ball and fell into the arms of his son, William, who was one of the marines. John Pitcairn died in Boston from his wound.

General Howe Esq.ʳ
of the Conecticut and comander Army in America.

Primary Source:
William Howe

This is an engraving of William Howe. Howe and his brother, Richard, served as Members of Parliament. They opposed the British government's policies toward the colonies in the 1760s and 1770s.

Thinking About the Source:

What is the physical setting of this image?

What, if any, words can you see?

If this image were created today, what would be different?

Abigail Adams (1744–1818)

Abigail Adams read a great deal. She felt that women should get an education. Abigail married John Adams in 1764. In 1774, John left for Philadelphia to serve in the **Continental Congress**. He remained there for ten years, which included the entire time of the Revolutionary War. When John was away, Abigail managed the family farm and business.

The White House was not completely finished when John and Abigail Adams moved in. Abigail used one of the rooms to hang clothes to dry.

"Remember the Ladies"

John and Abigail wrote letters to each other throughout the times they were apart. Their letters are now a valuable historic record. Abigail Adams sometimes spoke to her husband about women's rights. When John Adams and others were working on the Declaration of Independence in 1776, Abigail asked him to "remember the ladies." She and John had five children, including John Quincy, who would later become president. Abigail Adams became the first lady in 1797, when her husband John was elected the second president of the United States.

Lydia Darragh (1729–1789)

The Darraghs were Quakers. Quakers usually stayed out of war because of their religious beliefs. For this reason, the British thought the Darragh house was a safe place to hold meetings and discuss their plans. On the night of December 2, 1777, Lydia overheard their plan to attack Washington's Continental Army, which was about 13 kilometers (8 miles) away. Darragh obtained a pass to visit a nearby mill to get flour. Once out of the city, she was able to pass a message to warn Washington. When the British encountered the Continental Army, it was ready. They were forced to return to Philadelphia.

Lydia Darragh came from Ireland to live in Philadelphia.

ANN BATES (1748–1801)

Not all women involved in the American Revolution were **Patriots**. Ann Bates and her husband were **Loyalists**. Ann Bates helped the British by spying on the Continental Army while selling items to camp followers (women and children who followed the armies). After the war, Bates moved to England along with many other Loyalists.

Elizabeth Freeman (Mum Bett) (c.1742–1829)

Mum Bett and her sister were slaves. They served a family named the Ashleys in Massachusetts. One day, Mrs. Ashley tried to hit Mum Bett's sister with a shovel. Mum Bett stepped in and took the blow. She then left the house and refused to return. She had heard people talking about the idea that all people were born equal and free. Mum Bett found a lawyer who helped her try to get her freedom. A county court in Massachusetts freed Bett. This was a first step that led to the **abolition** of slavery in Massachusetts. Mum Bett took the last name "Freeman" after she won her freedom.

Sybil Ludington (1761–1839)

In April 1777, British General William Tryon invaded Connecticut. A messenger was sent to the Ludington house to tell Colonel Ludington to gather his **militia** troops. The colonel had to remain at home to gather any militiamen who came in. The messenger from Danbury was exhausted and could not ride any farther. The colonel's daughter, Sybil, who had just turned 16, rode through the night to tell the militiamen to meet at their house. By dawn, most of the militiamen were gathered and ready to march.

Sybil Ludington rode 64 kilometers (40 miles) on horseback through rough countryside during the night to alert the local militiamen.

The legend of Molly Pitcher comes to life here, where she is pictured firing a cannon at the Battle of Monmouth.

THE LEGEND OF MOLLY PITCHER— MARY LUDWIG HAYS MCCAULEY (1754–1832)

It was a hot day at the Battle of Monmouth in June 1778. Mary Hays (known as Molly) carried water in a pitcher to give to the thirsty men and to cool down the cannons. According to legend, when her husband was killed by enemy fire, Molly took over the cannon. Many historians doubt the legend.

However, "Molly Pitcher" may have been a nickname for all the women who carried water to help cool down the cannons. Margaret Corbin's story is similar, but definitely true. She helped her husband load a cannon while defending Fort Washington in New York in November 1776. Margaret stepped into her husband's place after his death to load and fire the cannon. She was wounded in the battle.

Betsy Ross (1752–1836)

The story goes that George Washington and two other men approached Betsy Ross in her shop one day in 1776. They wanted her to make a flag with stripes and stars. Supposedly, Ross suggested the stars have five points. She then made the first Stars and Stripes flag. Experts disagree on whether or not this story is true. However, it is known that Betsy Ross made many flags at her home in Philadelphia.

Deborah Sampson (1760–1827)

Women were not allowed to join the army during the Revolutionary War. In 1782, Deborah Sampson pretended to be a man and enlisted in the Continental Army. Deborah was wounded twice and was able to keep her secret. When she caught a fever, however, she had to be taken to a hospital. The doctor soon realized Deborah was a woman. She had fought and earned the respect of her fellow soldiers on the battlefield. Deborah was **honorably discharged** in 1783.

Betsy Ross ran her flag-making business for over 50 years.

Phillis Wheatley (c. 1753–1784)

Phillis Wheatley was kidnapped and forced into slavery when she was about eight years old. John Wheatley bought her in Boston in 1761. The Wheatley's taught Phillis to read and write English and Latin. She began writing poetry at age 12. A collection of her poems was published in London in 1773. It was the first book published by a black American. Wheatley was freed from slavery that same year.

Martha Washington (1731–1802)

When Martha Dandridge was 26 years old, her husband, Colonel Daniel Parke Custis, died suddenly. She married Colonel George Washington in 1759. Martha often stayed with her husband at his army headquarters. She spent the long winter at Valley Forge with George, helping him out and working to cheer up the men. Martha Washington became the first First Lady of the United States when George Washington was elected the first president.

Martha Washington took charge of George's meals in the winter camp at Valley Forge.

Timeline

1754–1763	French and Indian War
1764	Sugar Act passed
1765	Stamp Act passed
1765	Quartering Act passed
	Sons of Liberty formed
1766	Stamp Act repealed
	Parliament passes Declaratory Acts
1767	Townshend Acts passed
1768	British troops in Boston
1770	Boston Massacre (March 5)
1772	Boston Committee of Correspondence formed
1773	Tea Act passed
	Boston Tea Party (December 16)
1774	Intolerable Acts passed
	First Continental Congress meets
1775	Paul Revere and William Dawes warn colonists that the British are coming
	Battles of Lexington and Concord (April 19)
	Second Continental Congress meets
	George Washington appointed commander of Continental Army
	Battle of Bunker Hill (June 17)
	Defeat at Quebec (December 30)
1776	Thomas Paine writes Common Sense
	Siege of Boston ends
	Declaration of Independence signed (July 4)
	New York falls to the British
	Battle of Trenton, New Jersey (December 26)
1777	Battle of Princeton, New Jersey (January 3)
	Fort Ticonderoga falls to the British (July 5)
	Battle of Bennington (August 16)
	Battle of Brandywine (September 11)

	Philadelphia falls to the British (September 26)
	Battle of Germantown (October 4)
	Battle of Saratoga (October 7)
	British General Burgoyne surrenders (October 17)
	Congress passes Articles of Confederation (November 15)
	Winter of Washington's army at Valley Forge
1778	France declares war and joins the Patriot cause
	Battle of Monmouth Courthouse (June 28)
	Savannah captured by the British (December 29)
1779	George Rogers Clark captures Vincennes (February 25) in the Western frontier
	Naval battle of John Paul Jones's *Bonhomme Richard* against the British warship *Serapis* (September 29)
1780	Charleston, South Carolina, falls to the British (May 12)
	Battle of Camden (August 16)
	Battle of Kings Mountain (October 7)
1781	Battle of Cowpens (January 17)
	Articles of Confederation adopted by the states (March 1)
	Battle of Guilford Courthouse (March 15)
	Battle of Eutaw Springs (September 8)
	Cornwallis and the British surrender at Yorktown, Virginia (October 19)
1783	Treaty of Paris signed, ending the war (September 3)
	Continental Army disbanded, and Washington retires from the military
1785	Congress establishes dollar as official currency
1786	Shay's Rebellion
1787	Northwest Ordinance
	Constitutional Convention meets and Constitution signed (September 17)
1788	Federalist Papers
	Constitution is ratified
1789	First meeting of Congress
	George Washington sworn in as first president
1791	Congress adopts the Bill of Rights as the first ten amendments to the Constitution

Glossary

abolition when a law or system is officially ended

Bill of Rights part of the U.S. Constitution that is a list of the rights of U.S. citizens, such as freedom of speech and freedom of religion

cavalry part of an army that fights on horses

colony area that is under the political control of a more powerful country that is usually far away

commodore high rank in the navy, in charge of a group of ships

Continental Congress group of men who represented the thirteen colonies during the time of the Revolutionary War; its members are often called the "Founding Fathers"

delegate someone elected or chosen to represent a group of people

Federalist Papers writings that were published in newspapers to promote the official approval of the U.S. Constitution

French and Indian War name for fighting that took place 1754–1763 in North America between the French and the British

frontier area where not many people have lived before and not much is known about; the borderlands of a country

honorably discharged let out of the military after having served with honor

House of Burgesses in Virginia, first group of people elected to make laws in colonial America

Intolerable Acts name colonists gave to the Coercive Acts of 1774, which included several acts

Louisiana Territory land purchased from France by President Thomas Jefferson in 1803; it included a huge amount of land, from New Orleans up to present-day Montana, which doubled the size of the United States

Loyalist person who remained loyal to Great Britain during the Revolutionary War

marine soldier trained to fight both on land and at sea

militia group of people who act as soldiers but are not part of the permanent, professional army

Monroe Doctrine idea of President James Monroe that European countries should stay out of the western affairs of North and South America

mutiny when soldiers or sailors refuse to obey the person in charge and instead try to take control themselves

negotiate discuss and decide on an agreement between people or countries

Parliament main lawmaking group in Great Britain

Patriot person who supported independence from Great Britain during the Revolutionary War

rebellion organized attempt to change the government or leadership of a country by using violence

siege situation in which an army surrounds a place to try to gain control of it or force someone out of it

Sons of Liberty secret groups formed in the colonies before the Revolutionary War that included people who protested British taxes and supported independence from Great Britain

Stamp Act act in 1765 that required a tax to be paid when paper documents were made or sold; each item had to be stamped as proof that the tax had been paid

Sugar Act act in 1764 that taxed molasses shipped to colonial ports and prevented the colonies from importing molasses from other countries

survey examine and measure an area of land and record the information on a map

Tea Act act in 1773 that made the East India Company the only company allowed to sell tea in the American colonies, with Parliament collecting a tax on it

Townshend Acts acts in 1767 that placed taxes on items brought into the colonies, including paper and tea

treason crime of being disloyal to a person's country or government

tyranny cruel or unfair control over other people

War of 1812 war between the United States and Great Britain fought from 1812 to 1815

Find Out More

Books

Anderson, Laurie Halse. *Independent Dames: What You Never Knew About the Women and Girls of the American Revolution*. New York: Simon & Schuster Children's, 2008.

Murray, Stuart. *American Revolution*. New York, DK Children, 2005.

Wales, Dirk. *Twice a Hero: The Stories of Thaddeus Kosciuszko and Casimir Pulaski: Polish American Heroes of the American Revolution*. Winnipeg, Manitoba: Great Plains, 2007.

Websites

http://www.historyforkids.org/learn/northamerica/after1500/history/revolution.htm
This site, run by Kidipede, provides all kinds of links discussing different ideas and events of the Revolutionary War.

http://www.pbs.org/ktca/liberty/
This PBS site discusses the American Revolution and matches a TV series aired by PBS called "Liberty! The American Revolution," which is also available on DVD.

http://kids.yahoo.com/directory/Around-the-World/Countries/United-States/History/Colonial-Life-(1585-1783)/American-Revolutionary-War
This Yahoo! Kids site has useful links to other sites that discuss the Revolutionary War.

DVDs

Liberty! The American Revolution (DVD). Hosted by news anchor Forrest Sawyer and narrated by Edward Herrmann. PBS DVD Video, 1997.

The Revolution (DVD). History Channel DVDs, 2006.

Index